For my children
Yehonadav, Marom, Eliya & Aviad.

Introduction

Why is it so difficult for an alcoholic to stop drinking? It seems as though it would be easy enough just to quit and be done with it. Why do alcoholics continue to drink even though they know that it is hurting themselves and the people around them that they love? Why do so many alcoholics quit for a short period of time and then fall right back into it?

In order for me to overcome the hold that alcohol had on me, I had to dive deep into the inner workings of my mind to find the underlying reasons for my addiction and resolve them.

In this book, I tell the story of my alcoholism and the thought loops that held me in place.

A Personal Note

I write this from a place of pure love, understanding, acceptance, and compassion for those of you who struggle with this addiction. I know the depths of the pain and suffering that accompany alcoholism. If you are reading this, it means that you are on the right path by reaching out and searching for an answer. This is the first step towards freeing yourself.
Know that you can do this and that you are worth it. You are the only one who can do it for yourself. You are stronger than you think.
One foot in front of the other, one day at a time...

Inside the Mind of an Alcoholic

Thought Loops That Keep Us in Place
A Personal Story by Shoshanna Bat Shachar
Schmalz

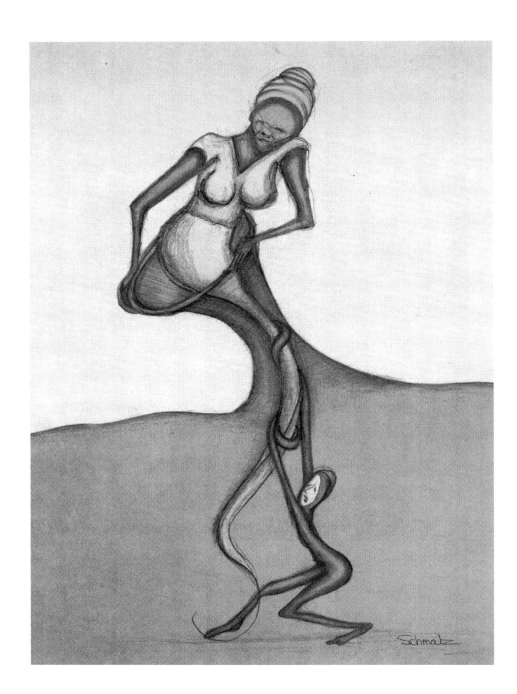

My Personal Story

Alcohol has played a significant role in my life since my earliest memories. While I was growing up, my parents would regularly consume alcohol in the evenings and during social gatherings. My mother started to really have a problem with alcohol addiction when I was about twelve. She would drink every evening. She wasn't a mean alcoholic, rather an over-loving alcoholic. She would want me to sit with her while she rambled on, slurring her words. Half of the time, I had no idea what she was talking about and often she would forget what she was talking about mid-sentence or repeat herself endlessly.

I felt a deep emptiness and sorrow. Powerless to help her, I started to avoid her when she was drinking. It disgusted me. When I was a young child, she was a loving and caring mother, but as an alcoholic, there was nothing there but a hollow shell of herself.

She would roll out of bed late in the morning and begin drinking straight away. Early during the day, I could still have a meaningful conversation with her, but by mid-afternoon, she wasn't there anymore.

The house reeked of vodka and was always a mess. Many times I had to help her just to walk to the bathroom. She fell a lot, and would get hurt often. My Younger siblings caught the brunt of this during their early childhood. My two older brothers and I helped take care of the younger ones as much as we could, but they were often left to fend for themselves. My siblings and I began to disregard her. I thought that she was going to die and I accepted it.

There was a lot of shame that came with having an alcoholic parent. I didn't want anyone to know and always tried to hide it. I wouldn't bring people home, fearing they would judge me and my family.

In 1999 my mother went through a two week dry-out program and has been alcohol free since. She has returned to being herself, a loving and supporting mother and grandmother. She lives knowing that alcohol is simply not an option for her.

My father always drank, but he's a different type of alcoholic. He has more control but alcohol definitely plays a role in his life.
Addictions run in families, and many people in my family line, on both sides, have struggled with addiction.

We grew up with little means, and we were always moving, so there is no place that I ever felt as though I came from. I was born in Jerusalem to American parents, and when I was two we moved to the States. We lived in Montana, Oregon, Arkansas and California. When I was twelve we came back to Israel and moved several times within Israel. Although our house was full of love, as a child, I always had an underlying feeling of unworthiness, and I never really felt like I belonged anywhere. I had an illusive belief that people that had means were happy and didn't have worries.

Overall, I had a wonderful childhood experience, full of love, inspiration and adventure, but underlying it is the story of the role that alcohol played in my life.

At fourteen, I dropped out of school and started working. I was drafted into the IDF before my eighteenth birthday, and after completing my service and being released back into civilian life, I felt lost and like I had nowhere to go, I didn't want to go back home. I married before my twentieth birthday and had two children by the age of twenty-two. In retrospect, I understand that it was the way to escape and find security.

My addiction to alcohol started gradually, and by all logic, I should have known better. Alcohol was a natural outlet for me because it was familiar and comfortable. As I fell into alcoholism, I knew what I was doing even in the earliest stages.

When I was twenty-nine, my husband and I moved our family from Israel to the suburbs of Chicago with $1,200 to start a new life. For the first couple of years in the States, my husband was a long-distance truck driver, and I was left alone with two young children most of the time. One evening, a few weeks after we got there, I went into the supermarket and saw the beer aisle. I thought that it would be really nice to have a beer and relax, so I bought a six-pack. I think I had two beers that night, and it took the pressure off.

I drank every night after that until I finished them and repeated it a couple of weeks later.

When I got pregnant with my third child I stopped drinking. After my son was born, I began doing the same thing, even while nursing. I noticed that the amount that I was drinking was slowly increasing. Instead of two beers, I was having three to four beers a night when I drank, but at this point, I still wasn't drinking every night. After a year and a half, I was pregnant with my fourth child and stopped drinking again. I remember thinking that he was my savior from alcoholism, yet almost as soon as he was born, I began drinking again (while nursing).

Between the births of my two youngest children, my husband and I opened a business, and success was almost immediate. Yet, with the success came many long work days and constant stress. I was daily juggling work with taking care of the kids and home. I was also in a very emotionally and verbally abusive relationship with an extremely controlling husband.

At that point, our marriage was falling apart and I didn't care about his feelings toward my alcohol abuse or anything else. There was no love or compassion, I was far from my family and had no friends. I knew that I was falling into alcoholism, but the relief that it gave me was stronger than the fear of alcoholism. I still believed I had control.

Slowly, I started to crave alcohol, like a burning sensation in the back of the throat or larynx. I knew that I had a problem but denied the extent of it, or the damage that I was causing to myself and my family. Now, I realize that I could not see the effect that I was having on my children because I dismissed my importance or the impact that I had on their lives. I disregarded my importance as a mother. I didn't think it was a big deal.

Alcoholism is Progressive

Gradually, my evening drinking started earlier and earlier in the day, sometimes even before I left work. Many times, I picked my kids up from daycare after I had already had a couple of drinks. I would be very careful not to get too close to anyone so that they would not smell it. Driving drunk was routine for me, and I made all my plans around my drinking.

I would drink until I fell asleep every night and that was usually on the couch. In the morning, I would walk around the house collecting empty and half-full cans that I had misplaced the night before. I hid the cans under other trash in the garbage bin so no one would see how many there were. Many times, in the morning, I would not remember what happened the night before. I pretended to know what the conversation was about while trying to remember or figure out the situation.

I tried to stop drinking by myself many times. I would stop for a few days at a time but the pull was too strong, so I would fall back into it. These falls were devastating to me; I felt guilty and like a failure. In all, I was drinking for around seven years.

The Beginning of the End

At thirty-six, I started to look in the mirror. I had reached success by many people's standards. I had an unlimited platinum credit card, and I could buy whatever I wanted. I had a fancy car, a big house in the suburbs and a successful business. But my life was empty. What was it all worth if nothing brought me pleasure?

At that time, I weighed close to three hundred pounds because of the excess calories, the alcohol, working all the time and being in a bad marriage. As a child, I had connected happiness to money, and I found it to be a myth. I had to make a change. I knew that there had to be more meaning to life. I didn't want to die this way, and I knew that I had more to give to my children and myself.

I decided to leave everything.

I separated from my husband and moved back to Israel to be close to my family. I could see the worry in my mother's eyes. She helped me find a therapist, but I still couldn't find the strength to quit. I didn't want to leave my children and go to rehab. I tried again to quit on my own but fell back after ten days.

My husband also moved back to Israel and took formal action to try to take my kids away from me, which he later canceled; he didn't want the separation. I was scared, and the shame was immense. I didn't want anyone from the outside to know. I remember my therapist telling me that one day, after I recover, I will not be ashamed anymore and that I would be able to talk about it openly. I did not believe her.

Rock Bottom and Rehab

One morning, I woke up and couldn't find two of my four children, and I had no idea where they were. I was supposed to get them ready for school, and they weren't there. I had to wake up my sixteen-year-old son to ask him what had happened the night before. The lost look and look of total disgust in his eyes as he told me, changed something in me. This was my wake up call, my rock bottom.

My therapist helped me find a closed dry-out facility and within a couple of weeks, I checked in. The thought of giving up alcohol scared me, but I made the decision that I was going to surrender myself to the care of others. I would simply do whatever they told me to do. I obviously didn't know how to do it on my own, so I gave myself to them trustingly. It felt like I was letting go of all control in my life.

My mother and daughter accompanied me and helped me sign in. I remember joking around with the doctors. When my mother and daughter left, and I walked into the ward, I saw people sitting in a circle in a group meeting. They looked ragged and worn, and a strong sense of flight came over me. I wanted to run. I felt like I didn't belong there among those people. I felt that I was not like them, but I was. For a second, the thought crossed my mind that I could still catch my mother in the parking lot, but I knew that I couldn't leave. I needed this, so I stayed.

We had group meetings twice a day along with lots of chores. It was not fun, and mostly, I remember being bored. Nearly all the people that were in rehab with me had been there many times prior. This made me realize that it is not a quick fix and that relapse is a real possibility. Almost daily, people were signing themselves out so they could go and drink. One of the ladies in my room had been to rehab seven times. I stayed and completed the two-week program.

When I got back home, I still struggled with cravings, especially during the first few days. My children gave me strength. They acted as though they had gotten their mother back "fixed." I remembered getting my mother back, and how wonderful it felt. They did not fathom that I could still fall back into drinking and I could not let them down. So, I stayed strong and adopted my mother's way of thinking, alcohol is simply not an option for me, no matter what. As the time passed it got easier and easier.

Understanding the Underlying Reasons for My Addiction

In order to overcome the hold that alcohol had on me, I had to go deep within myself to untangle and sort through tightly-intertwined emotions and beliefs. This is what I know to be true, based on my own experience with alcoholism.

My alcoholism sprouted from emotional agony caused by my inability to cope with my internal emotions. It may seem as though outside circumstances cause alcoholism, but they do not. Alcohol is a vice, a symptom of emotional distress. I was stuck in constant loops of self- pity, blame, shame, self-hatred, guilt, and denial. I was oblivious to these loops. Because I was unaware of these thought processes, they were impossible for me to change.

Self-Pity and Blame

Self-pity can be very comforting. When you pity yourself, you are just blaming others and outside circumstances for your situation. Feeling sorry for yourself is the opposite of taking responsibility. If you are feeling sorry for yourself, then you are under the false pretense that you are the victim of outside circumstances and of other people's behaviors. In other words, you don't feel as though you have control or power in the situation.

One of the biggest lessons that I received from my alcoholism is that when I blame others for the situation I am in, I have to wait for others to change in order for the situation to change. When I realized that I am the only one that can make a change in my life, then I quit blaming others and took back my power.

Others can only do to me that which I allow them. If others treat me poorly and I stay, then I am allowing them to treat me this way. It is not that they are to blame; they are only doing what they know how to do based on their own internal dialogue. When I blame others, I am giving them power over my life.

Imagine your life as a car that doesn't stop and you choose which seat you want to sit in. You can choose to sit in the passenger's seat. You can choose the back seat or you can choose to be in the driver's seat. No matter what seat you choose, the car will still go. Imagine that you choose the passenger's seat and let someone else drive, but you continuously blame that person for taking turns that you did not want to take. As I let go of blame, I gained strength in the knowledge that I am in control of my life.

If I am in charge, then I am the only one that is responsible for my alcoholism, and I am the only one that can change the situation.

I took back the power in my life by letting go of blame and checking within myself what I needed to do in order to change the things that I wanted to change.

Shame

The shame experienced as an alcoholic, or any shame, stems from feeling less adequate than others. I felt like there was something wrong with me because I couldn't control my alcoholism. I was worried about people finding out, so I stopped being social and stopped putting myself in social situations altogether. The shame made me hide both emotionally and physically. Shame is one of the lowest vibrational emotions that you can feel. It is the opposite of self-worth. I was ashamed of who I was and what I did; I didn't feel worthy of anything or anybody. Even just going to the park with my children was emotionally difficult.

Self-Hate and Feelings of Inadequacy

Self-hate is extremely destructive. I hated myself and could not believe that another could love me. I felt as though I was not worthy of love. So I sought out a relationship of which I felt worthy and settled into a destructive marriage, staying there many years. In retrospect, I could not have had any true, meaningful relationship with this mindset. If you don't believe another can love the true you, you never really show them who your true self is. I was constantly hiding who I really was.

When you hate yourself, you find reasons to reinforce the self-hate in every situation. It is a constant dialogue in your mind. When I met new people, I would begin to imagine myself through their eyes. I became acutely aware of aspects of my personality and my body that I disliked the most. I would imagine that the other person was only seeing these aspects, and I couldn't just flow with conversation or act naturally. I would cut conversations and interactions with other people short.

When you see yourself in a certain way, you cannot believe that another sees you differently. When you hate yourself, you're really just giving up on yourself, and you do not feel like you deserve more than your lot, so you don't strive for better.

The cycle of self-hatred and feeling unworthy is one of the hardest cycles to break. When you think this way, you can only see that which reinforces this way of thinking. When someone compliments you, you may feel as though you are being patronized, but if somebody points out something that you did wrong, you will take it, own it, dwell on it and grow it. You beat yourself up over it and play the recording of how stupid you are over and over again, whereas those that believe in themselves and love themselves would not take it to heart. Rather, they would realize their mistake, learn the lesson and grow from it.

We are not born all-knowing; therefore, a person who does not make mistakes does not exist. There is the person who takes responsibility and learns the lessons from their mistakes, and there is the one who chooses not to learn the lessons, nor to accept responsibility, thereby dwelling in that place of blaming (including self-blame).

When you don't learn from a situation then you are likely to repeat it. Self-hate feeds and reinforces itself with every loop. The lower you feel, the harder it is to pull yourself up. This loop makes it very difficult to pull oneself out of alcoholism. You feel as though it doesn't matter anyway.

Guilt

Guilt was my constant companion as an alcoholic. I felt guilty about what I was doing to others, especially to my children. I felt guilty about what I was doing to myself. I felt guilty because deep down I knew better, and I knew that I was responsible, even though I was not consciously aware of it and outwardly blamed others and outside circumstances.

These loops of thought are self-feeding, hold you down and lock you in their grasp and constraining boundaries.

Not only was I having these negative dialogues within my own mind, but the people in my life, especially the people closest to me, were blaming me for my alcoholism as well. They didn't understand me. This made me go further into my own hell. This just made me hide myself from them more and live in complete self-isolation. Alcoholism is lonely.

My addiction to alcohol made my mind manipulate itself. It twists your truths and morals around in such a way that it changes the way you think about alcohol, justifying your drinking in order to satisfy the addiction. As an alcoholic, I would wake up in the morning and be disgusted with myself for drinking. Many times, I would swear to myself that I would never touch another drop of alcohol. I would look at myself in the mirror and tell myself that I'm going to stay connected to this feeling, and that I never want to drink again, but as the day progressed, my hatred and disgust would begin to fade and my mind would talk itself into drinking. I would tell myself that everybody has a drink in the evening and that I'm not going to hurt anybody by drinking. An alcoholic's mind tricks itself as the hour to drink approaches. I often compare what took place in my mind to Dr. Jekyll and Mr. Hyde. This is one of the hardest things to overcome. You can't trust your own self.

The addiction to alcohol is progressive and intensifies with time. The longer the alcoholism is allowed to flourish, the deeper the roots and the harder it is to break. The earlier it is caught, the easier it is to overcome.

There will not be a point in the future that it will be easier than it is at this very moment. What started out as casual drinking slowly matured into the demon of alcoholism taking over my life. As it spread through my mind, it slowly engulfed every component of my life, shadowing it and choking out the love, happiness and meaning of every aspect. Alcoholism replaced everything positive with guilt, indifference, impatience and bitterness. It's numbing. I lost love for life, for self, for others and a sense of purpose.

I quit enjoying my children and my home. I lost hobbies and friends. Nothing had meaning for me anymore but the alcohol. I became my best and only friend. It feels like a warm blanket that drowns out the pain. But this is an illusion, because alcoholism brings with it far more pain than can ever be imagined, and most of the pain that I was trying to kill was brought on by the alcohol itself.

Understand that we are each born individual and unique, and we all come into the world the same, as equals. Each of us is worthy of love and understanding. We lose this belief because of experiences we have along the way and things that we are told in life.

Denial

Denial or partial denial of the addiction is why it can take so many years to get help. You cannot see the extent of your problem (or don't want to), and you tell yourself that you can quit anytime if you really want.

To make any kind of true and lasting recovery, you must first admit to yourself that you have a problem. This can be extremely difficult to do because once you admit that you have a problem, you must take responsibility for it. The alternative is to give in to the alcohol knowingly.

Breaking Point, Rock Bottom

In order to break the denial and get the full lesson needed to overcome alcohol addiction, you must first descend into your own personal rock bottom. Rock bottom is different for each person. It is such a low point that you cannot go lower. You feel as though you are choosing between life and death. You cannot lie to yourself any longer. You have to face the truth and admit to yourself that you have a problem. You realize that this is what your life has become and that you may end it this way.

This breaking point is usually triggered by a traumatic moment or a series of events brought on by alcohol. When you reach this breaking point, you are faced with a life or death choice. Either you admit it, take responsibility and reach out for help, or you admit it and give in to the addiction. In both cases, you cannot deny it to yourself any longer. Those who choose the latter, perish. This is because you quit resisting and give in to the alcohol knowingly. You accept it as your fate.

For me, the breaking point was when I woke up in the morning and could not find two of my four children, one of whom was six at the time. My children were fine. My daughter, who was fifteen at the time, left to sleep at her grandparents' house. My six-year-old had called his father the night before to come and get him because he was hungry, and there was no one there to feed him because I was "asleep."

Admitting That You Have a Problem

Once you admit to yourself that you have a problem, you must be able to admit it to others and ask for help. Asking for help can be one of the most difficult things to do. What I found is that once I asked for help, there was a huge weight lifted from me. I was not alone anymore, and I could lean on another for strength.

Another thing that I found is that people who were close to me knew I had a problem anyway, whether I had admitted it to them or not. You must be able to ask for and accept help.

The physical addiction to alcohol can be just as difficult to overcome as the mental addiction. Your body physically craves it and needs alcohol just to feel normal. Without alcohol your body shakes uncontrollably and you feel sick. You cannot physically function without it. You cannot move. The physical craving feeds your mental craving. I tried many times to break my addiction by myself, but I was unable. You cannot think rational thoughts while your body is craving alcohol, nor can you think rational thoughts while you are under the influence of alcohol, and these are your two constant states of being.

The physical addiction must be broken before you can begin the mental recovery. Knowing as an absolute truth that you are the only one who can pull you out of alcoholism is key. No one else has that power. The work is yours. But with saying this, I will also say that you cannot do it alone, and you do not need to do it alone. Reach out and find help. I still religiously continue group meetings and personal therapy.

The Importance of Therapy

Therapy is very important. When we are stuck in the destructive loops of thought, another's perspective can show us a different way of thinking and help us break the loop. I have a very talented and dedicated therapist, Adi, who slowly helped me work through my personal demons. She showed me rays of light that I did not see and planted seeds in my mind of other ways of living. With time and the right care, these seeds flourished.

Surround yourself with people that build you up and avoid those who do not.

Breaking the Cycle Through Inspiration

Understand that you cannot beat yourself up enough or put yourself down far enough to break the cycle of alcoholism. The further down you are, the weaker you are, the less power you have and the more likely you are to break. You can only inspire yourself out of alcoholism. The further you lift yourself up in your thoughts, the more power you gain, and the more worthy you feel. Worthy of change.

You can use positive affirmations to tell yourself a different story and reprogram your mind. Even if you don't believe it at first, "Fake it 'till you make it". If you tell yourself a new story every day, eventually you will believe it.

I am strong, I am capable, I am doing this, I love my life, and so on.

Meditate Daily.

Possibly the most important advice that I can give.

Meditation quiets the mind and allows you to connect back to your true self. Your true self is pure love and knows your worth.

You Can Do It and You Are Worth It

You can help yourself out of alcoholism by focusing on the positive things that you want in your life and the positive things that you want for yourself. Whatever it is that you focus on in your life is what expands. This is because the only moment in time that your life is happening is the current moment. The past is gone, and the future is not here. Everything that we dwell on in the past is inhibiting, and everything that we think of in the future is only a projection of our current thoughts and expectations. It is not actual. It is only an illusion.

If we can keep our current thoughts focused on positive things, our entire life experience will shift into a positive one. As we change our current thoughts, so will our projection and expectations of the future change. Our overall life experience will be tilted into the light rather than the darkness. Therefore, if you are focusing on not wanting to drink anymore, it is still the "drink" that is in focus; it is the subject of the conversation. What your thoughts are on is what is receiving airtime in your life and gaining power and momentum.

You are giving your addiction strength with every thought upon it. You must find things to focus on outside of the alcohol. Being in the clutches of alcohol can make it difficult even to see the smallest ray of hope to grab onto or find enjoyment in anything. Alcoholics who had a hobby or interest prior to alcoholism can visualize themselves enjoying them again. It may help to focus on a role model, someone that you can aspire to be like. Find a vision of yourself that you enjoy without the alcohol, how you would like to be. Hold that vision in your focus as much as you can.

When you feel yourself being pulled into the loops of your mind, pull yourself out and bring your new vision into focus. This mental process takes time and practice, but with perseverance you *can* do it.

If you look into your own mind as an observer and completely understand these loops of thought, you can slowly remove yourself from them, and if you can keep your thoughts positive, you can beat the addiction. I am not saying that it is not difficult to quit, but it is possible, and there is hope.

Through giving up alcohol, I was able to sort through my own personal demons and heal myself. I see my alcoholism as one of the greatest gifts that I was ever given.

As I write this, I am thirty-nine years old and nearly three years
alcohol-free.
(This is being published after ten years of being alcohol-free.)

I would like to thank all of those who have supported and encouraged me on this journey to my freedom and in the writing of this book.

Special thanks to my children - Yehonadav, Marom, Eliya and Aviad Benzaken and to my parents, Reuven and Elizabeth Schmalz. Thanks to my wonderful therapist Adi and to Nirit for advice and editing.

Find me on social media: YouTube, Facebook, Instagram and TikTok

@Schmalzling

Published 2023

Manufactured by Amazon.ca
Bolton, ON

35656217R00020